Danger and Despair

Sudden Death in Victorian Sheffield

Acknowledgements

Compiled, introduced and illustrated by Jane Horton.
Edited by Tanya Schmoller.
Researched by Tanya Schmoller, Alan and Sylvia Jackson, Professor Roy Newton, and Jane Horton for the Friends of the General Cemetery.

With thanks to James Buck for writing the story of Joseph Stead and the Dennis boys from news articles and Ruth Harman of the Victorian Society for finding the information about Leopold Lichtenthal.

FOGC gratefully acknowledges the support of Sheffield City Council Leisure Services, for their support in accommodating our research requests, and for the reprinting of news articles from the *Sheffield Mercury* and the *Sheffield and Rotherham Independent*.

Other sources: *The Sheffield Knife Book* by Geoffrey Tweedale, Hallamshire Press 1996.

ISBN 0-9539994-1-6

Introduction

Though the title of this book may attract you to its inevitably gruesome contents, remember that the people written about here were unfortunate victims of a society in which rapid industrial change led to a huge rise in health and safety risks for all, both in the workplace, on the streets and in the home. The General Cemetery itself came into being partly because of a recognition of the terrible health and safety risks associated with overcrowded graveyards in the growing city of Sheffield. Established 'at some distance in the countryside' in 1836, the General Cemetery was instigated by a group of prominent Nonconformists, each of whom contributed finance to the scheme, and resulted in the development of this unusually designed landscape, now recognized as of historic significance nationally. Now the final resting place of 87,000 people, this book holds a few details of a handful of those buried there.

As well as the increased risks to life in a fast growing city like Sheffield, there were the demands to adapt not just physically but psychologically to change. It seems that young men, as today, were most vulnerable to depression, and the General Cemetery holds the remains of many more young male suicide victims than women. Unfortunately those who committed suicide are rarely commemorated in memorials, perhaps because there is a preponderance of poor people among the suicides. Many appear to have been driven to suicide through fear of the workhouse, or at least, this fear weighed heavily upon their depressed minds. The lack of a safety net for the poorest sections of society is demonstrated through some of the tales represented here.

The Cemetery Company chose to bury most of the impoverished suicide victims together, and they are nearly all interred in a particular zone of the cemetery: at the bottom end of the hill, in front of the catacombs. It is likely that the shadowy base of the hill on which the cemetery is situated was seen as the least attractive part of the cemetery in which to be buried (cemeteries often ranked the cost of burials according to the position of the graves, and prominent elevated positions were inevitably the most expensive). This may also have been an aesthetic decision. The cemetery had certainly been deliberately designed with a sweeping line of catacombs leading the eye up the hill. Serried ranks of gravestones would have broken this impressive line, so what better place to bury those who, for sure, were not going to get a marker above their heads?

Extraordinarily, in this small sample of accidental deaths, there are two fathers and sons who died in separate accidents. In addition, John Pickering, whose death is described in this guide, had two siblings who were to die twenty years after his own terrible accidental death, in the Sheffield Flood of 1864. A double tragedy for these three families.

As for accidents: by far the most common cause of death by accident was fire, and the victims? Nearly all young girls, but some women too, in danger because of two principal factors: open fires and voluminous skirts. Among grown men the most common cause of accident seems to have been the *phaeton*, gig, or one-horse carriage, which seemed to tumble over on cobbled streets with alarming frequency. The story of the death of Ben Littlewood graphically demonstrates the lack of Victorian road safety: where were the rules of the road: the signs, signals and horns? It also illustrates the reality of no emergency response service for accidents. Tragically, one of the most gifted stonemasons working in the cemetery in mid-Victorian times, Theophilus Smith, nationally renowned for his wrought-iron work, abilities as a sculptor and also well known as an early photographer, was seriously injured by a carriage (he was a pedestrian) and never properly recovered. A close second to carriage accidents come industrial accidents, a reflection of the rapid industrialization of Sheffield, the lack of health and safety legislation, the power of employers over their workers, and the sometimes shocking working conditions.

It is sad to observe the number of drownings recorded in the burial records. One wonders how many people learned to swim in the course of their lives? Many more lives would have been saved if the victims had been able to swim. Overall it is striking how many of the lives lost that are described here would have been saved had these accidents happened in the twentieth century. Modern medicine, health and safety legislation and technological developments cushion us from the precariousness of existence. On the other hand, there are just as many instances of accidental death a century ago that have modern parallels. The death of Leopold, the young Russian showing off on his horse – just as a young inexperienced motorcyclist might today, children having an adventure somewhere they shouldn't have been playing with disastrous consequences – is almost as likely to happen today as in 1848. These deaths get us guessing about the ordinary people whose lives took a tragic turn. The accidental deaths recorded here are mostly male: 34 of out of 41. Such statistics have not changed, even if the causes have. Men and boys are much more likely to be injured in accidents than women and girls, even today. Another statistic consistent with today is reflected in the number of accidental deaths reported here: there are far more accidental deaths recorded in the labouring classes than among the well-to-do, a fact that unfortunately means some graves listed here have no headstone, as they are the graves of paupers.

In putting together this guide I debated rewriting the articles and obituaries discovered in the local press of the time. (Most articles are drawn from the *Sheffield and Rotherham Independent*, a few from the *Sheffield Mercury*, and one from a modern book about Sheffield Knives.) While a few reports have been rewritten because of the length of the stories, I have left the majority verbatim, as the language used to describe these tragic situations is in itself fascinating.

It is interesting to note that many of the inquests took place in pubs and taverns, presumably the nearest public house to the scene of the accident, and sometimes they even took place in shops. I also wonder at the number of inquests that took place: in particular Mr T. Badger comes up again and again as the man presiding over the inquests. He must have been tearing round Sheffield to get to all these tragic scenes, and probably justifies an investigation in his own right!

Something else you will notice is that many of the deaths reported in this book are from the 1830s and 1840s. This is because in this period of the cemetery's history, the Cemetery Company judiciously recorded not just the date of death, name of parents and address, but also the *cause* of death. This is fortuitous for local historians, and though not unique, it is unusual for a cemetery company to have recorded this information. This of course gives us a flag to go and investigate. Deaths with particularly tragic circumstances surrounding them are worth following up, because it is likely that news reports were written. Unfortunately, after 1856, the Cemetery Company ceased to record the cause of death, so an important clue to gain information about the individual buried was lost.

Finally, a word about locating the graves of the people in this guide. Those mentioned are from all walks of life. A majority of the people buried in this cemetery are in unmarked public, or pauper, graves; only the well-off could afford grand monuments, and the not-so-well-off struggled over years to save for funerals and a respectable stone to memorialize their loved ones. It cost £2 - £3 for a plot in the General Cemetery in 1836, and the cost of a simple monument would have been at least another £3 - £5. This compares with an average tradesman's monthly pay in 1836 of 12 shillings. So it is that only a few of the people whose deaths are described here were actually memorialized, and paths have been made to as many of their graves as possible. (Some are still inaccessible because of the thickness of the bramble that surrounds them or because the area has been fenced off for health and safety reasons.) If the text describes the gravestone as '*inaccessible*', do not attempt to locate it, it may be in a dangerous zone of the site.

One of the headstones I would like to have included in this guide, of John Cowlishaw, was destroyed in the 1978 Council clearance, along with at least five thousand other headstones. A note about him (still buried in the cemetery, though now with no marker) is included here in any case. As well as visiting the memorials that still stand, walk to the area of the cemeetery where Cowlishaw is buried, and the zone where the other suicide victims lie, and, contemplating their fates, enjoy the vistas through the cemeetery.

Note: burial plot numbers are refered to against each record, for the sake of completeness, and for the benefit of those eager to locate each plot. Plot maps of the General Cemetery are held by Sheffield City Archives and the FOGC.

People Guide

Caught up by the Flames

Sarah Goddard

On 18th May 1839 an inquest was held into the death of Sarah Goddard, aged nine years. 'The girl set herself on fire, by wafting the fire with her pinafore, and was so severely burnt as to cause her death.'
She is buried in a public grave B27 close to the Egyptian gate.

"The girl set herself on fire, by wafting the fire with her pinafore"

Emma Greaves

An inquest was reported on 3rd April 1841 'touching the death of Emma Greaves, aged seven years, daughter of Charles and Emma Greaves of Rockingham Street. She was admitted into the Infirmary on Saturday 27th March very severely burnt. It appeared she had been standing with her back to the fire in her father's house, and another girl was lighting some

paper by the fire, when the frock of the deceased was caught up by the flames.'
She is buried in a public grave B47 close to the Egyptian gate.

Charlotte Woolhouse

The death of Charlotte was reported on 3rd February 1855, from burn injuries. 'The child had been left by her mother at the house of a niece to play with her children. The children were placed in a room upstairs, and, while left alone, the deceased got on fire. The screams of the child alarmed the mother of her playfellows, and the flames were extinguished. The child was taken to the infirmary, where she died.'
Charlotte is buried in a public plot number F129, in the furthest corner of the cemetery in a very inaccessible area.

Susannah Sharpe

Susannah lived with her husband near the Lady's Bridge, and died on 13th February 1841 as a result of stooping down with her back to the fire, to look after her child. Her clothes accidentally caught fire and she was so severely burned that she died.
Susannah coincidentally shares a single public grave plot with Emma, whose death is recorded above, plot number B47. There are a total of sixty-one burials in this single plot.

Sarah, Emma, Charlotte and Susannah are four of the many young girls and women buried in this cemetery who died as a result of their skirts catching fire. Incredibly, in the nineteenth century, after childbirth, burning was the second most common cause of death among females.

Sodden Corpses

William and Thomas Dennis

On Sunday 8th October 1848, the bodies of two drowned boys were dragged from the waters of the River Don, not far from Lady's Bridge. Some thirty minutes before this tragic outcome, a watchman had raised the alarm after seeing 'the caps of the unfortunate youths floating on the top of the water'. Would-be rescuers set out on a raft to search the river - others furnished themselves with hooked poles and moved along the banks dragging the waters as they went; but this frantic activity availed nothing - save the recovery of two sodden corpses.

William Dennis, aged sixteen years and his younger brother Thomas, eleven, had, that morning, set out from the parental home in Fitzalan Square. They had permission from their father, to 'go to see the arch that had fallen in Sheaf yard.' Before his sons had left to see the spectacle, Joseph Dennis, a tailor of Baker's Hill, had cautioned them not to approach the river. This warning was addressed particularly to Thomas, the younger son, who may have been charged with the safety of his brother William who, though older, was described at the inquest as being 'rather weak of intellect'. Despite giving their father assurances to the contrary, the boys disobeyed his instruction and attempted to cross the Don, but they were warned off by a watchman.   On this occasion, the brothers pretended to leave the area of the Wicker, but doubled back and tried to cross the river again; but, once more, they gave up when spotted by the watchman. The boys' third and fatal attempt to cross the river was observed by a boy named George Machin, who later gave evidence to the inquest.   It is clear from Machin's account that Thomas was the prime mover in the tragic events which unfolded. The witness described watching from the opposite bank as Thomas urged a clearly fearful William to enter the river. That the feeble-minded boy was extremely anxious at that prospect, is apparent in Machin's observation that Thomas twice crossed the river by himself, going back-and-forth, as if to show his reluctant brother that all would be well. This strategy eventually succeeded to the extent that William took Thomas's hand and led him into the waters of the Don. Machin watched them moving edgewise, hand-in-hand, closer and closer to the middle of the river, where fate was waiting to turn the final card. Machin saw the bigger, older boy slip into the river and the smaller boy follow. A man, attempting to cross at the same time, saw the boys carried away by the flowing water; he hastened to alert the watchman whose dismal discovery of the boys' caps set the futile rescue attempt in train.

On the evening of the day following these events, an inquest was held in the Wicker, at the Station Inn. The jury's verdict was that William and Thomas Dennis had met with 'Accidental death'. The following news report is dated14th October, 1848:
'The unfortunate brothers were interred in the same grave, at the Cemetery on Wednesday. Thousands of persons, sympathising with the bereaved parents, witnessed the sad spectacle. We understand the family attend the Nether Chapel, and that the Rev. Thomas Smith will preach a sermon in reference to this distressing event next Sunday evening.'
They are buried in an inaccessible plot in the corner of the cemetery, F127.

Alfred Atkinson

The following news report appeared on 2nd February 1850: 'A fatal accident occurred in the forenoon on the large dam of the Water Company, in the Dam House, Crookes Moors, to Mr. Alfred Atkinson, son of Mr. S Atkinson, secretary to the Sheffield Reform Society and the Freehold Land Society. The deceased, who was passionately fond of skating, went upon the ice about ten in the forenoon and was skating round the dam. He had gone safely on two sides, but on the third the ice broke and he fell into the water. He endeavoured, fruitlessly, to cling onto the unbroken ice, and before any aid could be extended to him he disappeared. The ice was so dangerous, having been broken near the same place the day before, that it was necessary to construct a raft before any effective measures could be taken to recover the body, which was about three hours in the water. The deceased was a very fine young man, in his nineteenth year, and his untimely death has plunged the family into deep affliction.'
Alfred is buried in plot number W132, and his gravestone lies flat on the ground, on the second row in along the path from the centre junction to the Nonconformist chapel on the left side, one third of the way along the path.

Thomas Binns

Reported on 21st August 1847, was a story headed *Young Man Drowned in Chatsworth Park*. 'We regret to have to announce a fatal accident, which occurred at Chatsworth Park, the seat of his Grace, the Duke of Devonshire, on Wednesday last, to a young man, named Thomas Binns, aged 21, who was the driver of one of his mother's (Mrs. Jemima Binns) cabs. It appears that he, with a young man, named Thompson, the driver of another cab, had taken a party over to Chatsworth, and after putting up their horses at Baslow, walked into the Park. Near Queen Mary's Bower, they stripped, with the intention of bathing in the river Derwent, which passes through the grounds. Thompson, who had several times bathed at the place, cautioned young Binns, who could not swim, to keep to the side, as in the centre of the stream it was very deep. They got into the water at a shallow point, but it appears that Binns, neglecting the precaution of his companion, was crossing over to the other side of the stream, when he got out of his depth and sank. Thompson, who was not a good swimmer, dare not venture to follow him, but called to some gentlemen, who were playing cricket near, one of whom came to the spot, and jumped in the water, to Binns' assistance. He dived several times without being able to meet with him, and when at last found, it was not until a quarter of an hour had elapsed, when he was quite dead. The melancholy bereavement will be severely felt by his mother, to whom, since the death of her husband, a few years ago, by a coach accident, he has been of great assistance.

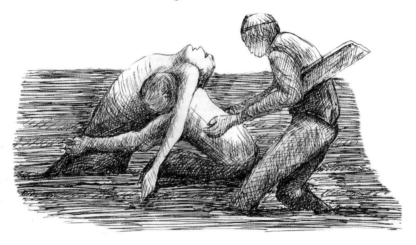

"When at last found, it was not until a quarter of an hour had elapsed"

A report on the death of Thomas's father is also included in this guide. Both are buried in plot H 169. Their gravestone, a chest tomb, is six plots to the left of the path leading up the hill to the Cemetery Office, three plots further up the hill from the retaining wall end. The inscription to Thomas reads: 'In life respected, in death lamented'. Unusually, Thomas's mother, following the death of her husband, and then son, on top of caring for a large family, took on the management of the family hackney cab business. She is recorded as 'cab, plain and figured hearse and mourning coach proprietress'. On her gravestone are the following words: 'She looketh well to the ways of her household and eateth not the bread of idleness'. Jemima lived to age sixty-four and died on 24th April 1868. The gravestone also records the death of her eldest daughter Charlotte, at the age of thirty.

Julia Hall

Reported on 24th August 1844. 'On Thursday evening a little girl, under three years old, the daughter of Mr. Hall, boot and shoemaker of Bow Street, was found drowned in the out-kitchen of her parents' house. It appeared the child was not seen after three o'clock in the afternoon, but no alarm was created as she was in the habit of going to a neighbour's house. About six in the evening, however, Mrs. Hall, going to the out-kitchen, found the child hanging over the edge of the maidening tub*, which contained water, and quite dead.'

* A maidening tub is a washing tub, in which clothes are pounded. Julia is buried in private plot B142, near the Egyptian gate.

John Naughton

A Man Drowned was reported on 24th February 1844. 'A body was taken out of the Twelve O'clock Wheel dam, in an advanced state of decomposition, which was discovered to be that of John Naughton, aged seventy-five. An inquest was held at the sign of the Twelve O'clock the same evening, when it appeared that the deceased, who was in receipt of parish relief, had left his lodgings in Oborne Street, Bridgehouses, on the 21st December, for the purpose of going to Wentworth House to ask for the dole given by Earl Fitzwilliam to the poor annually, on St Thomas's day. Though every enquiry had been made, he had not been heard of since, and there was no evidence to show how he had got into the river.

John Naughton is buried in public plot V86, in the clearing behind the James Nicholson memorial of a kneeling woman.

Darby Tule

An inquest was reported in the *Sheffield Mercury* on 22nd June 1839 that took place at Brightside Poorhouse into the death of Darby Tule, an Irishman, aged 30. 'It appeared from the evidence that the deceased came from a place called Straw Hill near Dublin, and had been in this country for six weeks. Being unable to obtain work, and having no money, he threw himself into the Sheffield Canal at Attercliffe, on Sunday morning. He was slowly taken out by some persons who had observed him jump into the water, and afterwards removed to the Poorhouse at Pitsmoor, where he received every attention. He began to have fits on Monday and died on Tuesday; death, there is no doubt, having been produced by immersion in water.'

Darby is buried in an unmarked public burial plot number B23, near the Egyptian gate.

Richard Robertshaw

A fatal accident was reported on 16th October 1847 at an inquest at the Fork Inn, Rockingham Street 'touching the death of Richard Robertshaw, a boy about four years old, who was drowned on Monday evening, by falling into a reservoir attached to the works of Mr. John Davenport, saw manufacturer. This reservoir, which is guarded only by a low paling, is used for the purpose of supplying the engine, and its high temperature is a source of great temptation to the boys employed on the works to indulge in a cheap warm bath, notwithstanding that they had been frequently reprimanded for doing so. On the evening in question, John Ibberson had been bathing. He had got out, and was dressing himself at the upper end of the yard, which is partitioned off by a pair of double gates, extending to the edge of the reservoir. The gates were locked, as the works were closed, and the deceased was endeavouring to get round the gates to Ibberson. He was twice removed by a youth named Howell, and on trying a third time, he fell into the water. The depth of the reservoir is near five feet, about eight inches of which is mud. Howell saw him fall, and gave an alarm, when Ibberson immediately plunged in after him, but, owing to the darkness of the evening, and the deceptive appearance of the water, nearly ten minutes elapsed before the body was found, when life was extinct. The jury returned a verdict of "Accidental death"; and to prevent similar accidents occurring they ordered Mr. Davenport to raise the fence which surrounds the reservoir to the height of five feet, within a fortnight, under a penalty of £10.'

Tragically Richard's father, also called Richard, died a grisly death, in an industrial accident, details of which are recorded in this guide. Both Richard and his father rest in private burial plot number L158, but their gravestone is currently inaccessible.

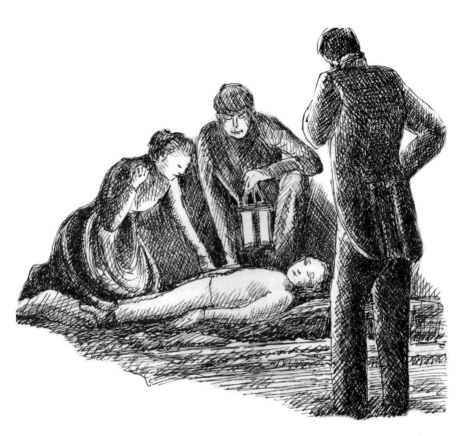

"Owing to the darkness of the evening, and the deceptive appearance of the water, nearly ten minutes elapsed before the body was found"

Violent Collisions

Joseph Stead

On a mid-winter afternoon, a fortnight before Christmas 1854, five Sheffield men set off together for a Sunday jaunt. One can paint a jolly seasonal card of their departure: in the foreground is a single horse; it is fastened between the shafts of an open, four-wheeled carriage. Surrounding the vehicle are five stout men in long winter coats. Each merry face is framed by top hat and muffler; and all are full of good cheer, having just emerged from the warmth and brightness of a town-centre hostelry. The host, Mr. John Hoole, inn-keeper of Silver Street Head, is one of the five; and he is about to drive them to their destination, another inn: the Grouse and Trout, at Redmires. Their outward journey may have taken them over Crookesmoor, and up Lydgate Lane, then around Tapton Hill. From there they would have got on to Sandygate Road; then straight on for Redmires. It has to be said that the vehicle, in which the five men travelled, was wholly inadequate to undertake such an expedition. It had only one horsepower and was therefore a version of the *Stanhope Phaeton.* These were regarded as a gentleman's town carriage, meant to carry three people only and dangerously unstable in the best of conditions. Why did these five Sheffielders venture on to the moors in such an unreliable mode of transport and at such a bleak time of year? The answer could well be that the laughs one has when dashing through the snow in a one-horse open *Phaeton* outweigh any fears of meeting a sticky end. We might speculate further and suggest that the men were pursuing a wager after an afternoon drinking session. The *Phaeton* pulled in around half-past four and the merry party tumbled into the welcoming Grouse and Trout. If evidence given at the inquest is to be believed, the five friends (two of whom were themselves publicans) showed admirable restraint in their drinking; they departed the inn, in the dark, at six o'clock, 'none of them having had more than a couple of glasses of spirits'.

As before, three crammed themselves in to the body of the carriage; a fourth man, Joseph Stead (steel founder of Ecclesall New Road), climbed up beside the driver Hoole, and the horse set off at a steady trot. For the next hour, over hills they go, laughing all the way. It was when the *Phaeton* reached the top of Lydgate Lane that a grim fate seized hold of the rein. As the carriage began its descent towards Crookes, the horse 'started off at a full gallop. Mr.Hoole endeavoured to stay it and, not succeeding in that, to steer it down the awkward lane as well as the darkness would permit. The vehicle had nearly upset several times, but kept up until it had arrived at a row of houses called Mount Pisgah when coming upon a gannister heap, it was dashed over and smashed into pieces.' The violence of the collision propelled Hoole and Stead up into the air: both landed on their heads with sickening force. When the three others, each of whom had escaped injury, picked up Stead, 'he was bleeding from the mouth and ears but was sensible. He said that he had no use of his legs and thought that he was killed. Hoole was unable to speak.' Deciding that their friend Stead was at least able to speak and was therefore in better fettle than Hoole, the three fortunate survivors of the crash packed the steel founder into a passing cab and sent him home in the charge of a boy. Hailing another cab they set off with Hoole to the South Sea Hotel, Broomhall.

Stead lapsed into unconsciousness during the cab journey. Neither the cab-driver, nor the boy, knew which number on Ecclesall Road was the Stead household. After wasting much time clip-clopping back-and-forth along the length of the newly-built road, the cab-driver decided his passenger needed his head mending with more than vinegar and brown paper, and turned his horse in the direction of Sheffield Town. Joseph Stead 'was attended by Mr.Walker, surgeon, Union Street, and seen by Dr.Law, but he never recovered his reason and died at four o'clock on Monday afternoon. There was a severe contused wound on the back of his head and it is believed the base of his skull was fractured, but no autopsy of the body was made.'

The inquest which followed Joseph Stead's violent and untimely death (he was thirty-one), was held at the Woodham Inn, Sheffield Moor. The driver of the *Phaeton,* John Hoole, was unable to attend the proceedings: having also suffered a fracture to his skull, he lay 'in a very dangerous state'. The coroner remarked that ' it did seem that proper attention had not been paid to the poor man, but there is this excuse: all parties would be so agitated that they would scarcely know what they were doing and might not think the deceased so much injured as he proved to be'. The jury returned a verdict of accidental death.

It is an irony that it was a heap of gannister that caused the Phaeton to throw Mr Stead; he was an iron founder and would have been entirely familiar with the close-grained siliceous stone found in the coal measures of northern England, and used for furnace linings.

On a mid-winter afternoon, a fortnight before Christmas 1854, five Shef-field men set off together for a Sunday jaunt.

Joseph Stead's grave (V3) can be seen by walking into the clearing where there is a modern headstone at the central junction in the cemetery. Just beyond the black headstone, in the undergrowth, is a flat horizontal stone memorializing Joseph.

Robert Bennett

A Fatal Street Accident was reported on 13th August 1853. On Tuesday evening, a child two years old, named Robert Bennett, whose parents reside in a court in Sydney Street, was accidentally killed whilst playing in the street. The boy had run into the street to play, at the same moment a cart belonging to Messrs Patrick and Garside, timber dealers, and in the care of Henry Radford, was passing the gateway of the court. Radford, being at the horse's head, could not see the child; but a woman named Taylor, witnessed the boy running towards the cart, and saw him fall between the hind legs of the horse and the cart wheel. Her screams alarmed the driver, and he pulled up before he passed over the child's head, but it was so much crushed by its pressure as to cause instant death. The child had not left its mother more than a minute before the accident, and she hearing the cart approach, was hastening to fetch him again when she saw his lifeless body lying in the road. No blame was attributable to the driver, as it was clear that he was driving steadily, and had perfect command of his horse. An inquest was held, when the jury, on hearing the circumstances, coincided in a verdict of accidental death.'

Robert was the son of James and Charlotte Bennett of Mycock's Yard, Sydney Street, and was buried in a public grave, burial plot number S107, close to the Dissenters' Wall.

Leopold Lichtenthal

Leopold died on 8th May 1849 aged 17 years, killed by a fall from a horse. The story of his death was revealed in a Sheffield newspaper which relates that Leopold was the only surviving son of a wealthy family in St Petersburg, his elder brother having died there of cholera in 1848. He was sent to England both to escape that disease and to learn English business methods, under the supervision of Mr. John Chambers, a Sheffield Solicitor. On the morning of Sunday 29th April 1849 he went to the Moorhead stables of Messrs Blackwell and West to collect a horse, ordered the previous day. He had boasted to a companion that he would show the Sheffield people how to ride. Requesting the best one available, he was told he could have Mr. West's own horse if he promised to ride it gently. The ostler was, therefore, most perturbed when he proceeded to put on spurs and warned Leopold that the horse would not stand them. The young man ignored his remonstrations and, spurring his mount, set off at a gallop.

Alas, disaster soon befell him, for it seems that his toes slipped from the stirrups which according to Russian custom he had had lengthened until he could hardly reach them. In his efforts to regain them he irritated the normally docile animal with his spurs. By the time they had reached Norfolk Street the horse was going at a furious rate and Leopold had lost control. As his hat flew off the door-keeper at the Methodist Chapel ran after him, urging him to hold on, but at Milt Street the unfortunate youth was thrown to the ground and suffered severe concussion.

He was taken to his lodgings in Glossop Road and was attended by several doctors. Although several times he partially regained consciousness, he finally died on Tuesday 8th May. Following an inquest held at the Beehive in Glossop Road he was buried on Saturday 12th May.

The burial register entry records that he was a mercantile clerk born in Brussels, the son of Herman Lichtenthal and Fanny. Cause of death was given as 'contusion of the brain'. Leopold's gravestone sits in the shade of a tree to the right of the Nonconformist chapel, at the top of a slope. It is ironic that later in 1849 there was a cholera outbreak in Sheffield.

James Hopkins

A news report of 15th May 1847: 'We regret to record an accident which caused the death of Mr. Hopkins, of Sheffield Baths, and severe and dangerous injury to Mrs. Hopkins. It appears that in consequence of the indisposition of Mrs. Hopkins, her husband had taken her out yesterday in a gig for an airing, and when near Rivelin Mill, the horse took fright, became unmanageable and ran away. The gig was overturned, Mr. and Mrs. Hopkins were thrown out, and he pitching upon his head died within 10 minutes

"The gig was overturned, Mr. and Mrs. Hopkins were thrown out"

at a neighbouring house to which he was conveyed. Mrs. Hopkins was brought home, but was found to be very severely, and we fear, dangerously injured.'

James and his wife Elizabeth are buried in private burial plot number G16. Our burial register shows that Mrs. Hopkins survived another two and a half years (she died of pneumonia in 1849). Their grave is inaccessible.

Ben Deakin Littlewood

The inscription on his gravestone reads *'who was killed on the Frogatt Edge Road by the overturning of a traction engine on April 10th 1882 aged twenty-one years'.'*

The news report was headed *Terrible Carriage Accident at Froggatt Edge*, with a sub-heading *Two Persons dead and two injured.* 'Yesterday's holiday, and the excursions into the country which formed so prominent a feature of the way in which it was spent, did not, unfortunately, come to an end without an accident, and that of a very terrible nature. The circumstances attending it are of a peculiarly painful character, for it resulted in the instant death of a young man just entering upon life, the almost immediate death of a beautiful young lady, pupil at a boarding school in Sheffield, beside more or less serious injury to two others of the party, and a painful shock to those who escaped personal injury. The accident was entirely due to a traction engine, and to what seems at present to be extraordinary conduct on the part of the driver. Between nine and ten o'clock yesterday morning, an open landau, drawn by a pair of horses, left Northumberland Road, the intention being to proceed to Tideswell. In it were Mr. George Staniforth, one of the chief officials at the works of Messrs Joseph Rodgers, Sons and Company Limited, Mrs. Staniforth, and two sons. The party also consisted of Mrs. Littlewood, wife of Mr. J.F. Littlewood, Taptonville; her son, Mr. B.D. Littlewood, Miss Mary Cook Smith, a young lady who was a boarder at Miss Boaler's school, Broomgrove; and Mademoiselle Julien, the French governess at the same establishment. The carriage was driven by Joseph Bailey….sitting with him was Mr. G Staniforth and the occupants of the rumble were Miss Staniforth and her cousin Mr. B.D. Littlewood. Until Frogatt Edge was reached the journey was devoid of anything but the pleasurable incidents which always accompany a drive into Derbyshire scenery, on such a splendid morning as that of yesterday. About a couple of hundred yards from the Grouse Public House, a little roadside inn, which stands on the right-hand side of the road, the driver and young Staniforth saw a traction engine and a couple of large trucks behind it, laden with coal. The engine was going down the road, and at that time on the left-hand side. Had it continued there no accident could possibly have happened, for there was plenty of room for the landau to pass, and Bailey naturally intended adopting that course. But when his horses were about to pass the second truck, the driver of the engine suddenly changed his course, and turned his engine towards the right-hand side of the road, thus bringing the engine into dangerous proximity to the carriage. Bailey and young Mr. Staniforth shouted as loud as they could to announce that the carriage was behind, but the driver didn't hear them, and still turned his engine towards the right-hand side. Bailey then saw that an accident was inevitable, and with the object of saving his carriage from being run into by the trucks, he drove his horses straight into a bank, which at this point is about eight feet high. The horses scrambled up part of the bank, dragging the carriage a few feet with them, but it then turned over, and all its occupants were thrown into the road. Just as this occurred, the last of the two trucks was passing by. It was therefore, nothing short of miraculous that the accident was not attended by even more lamentable circumstances than actually resulted, for the survivors found themselves thrown close to the truck and its wheels. As soon as the accident had occurred, the driver of the traction engine became aware that something unusual had happened, and at once pulled up his engine.

By this time those who were uninjured had managed to scramble out of danger, and to look about them to ascertain the result of the accident. A terrible sight then presented itself. Young Mr. Littlewood was seen lying just beneath the edge of one of the wheels of the truck, with a terrible wound in his head; Miss Smith was unconscious, with blood flowing from her nose; Mrs. Littlewood was lying with a serious wound on her head, and Mdlle. Julien with a fractured leg. The sufferers were immediately carried into a public house, which was only a few yards distant, for other vehicles were coming down the road, and their occupants lent ready assistance. But a hasty examination was sufficient to show that young Mr. Littlewood was dead; as regards Miss Smith, it was at first thought that she had only swooned, or had become unconscious by the shock; and in this belief brandy was applied and other restoratives resorted to. But though the young lady lived for a few minutes after being taken to the public house, consciousness could not be restored, and she passed away with scarcely a sigh, and with a face that almost wore a smile. Her dress did not show any signs of having been run over by the truck; and if this unfortunate young lady did not sustain an injury to the skull or brain in her fall, the supposition is that her death was caused by fright. The fact that her nose was bleeding lends some countenance to this supposition, for it is said that this was always the case when she laboured under unusual excitement or became frightened. As the carriage was uninjured, Bailey was instructed to endeavour to obtain the services of a surgeon, and with this object he drove to Baslow, to Middleton, and Eyam. A telegram was also dispatched to Sheffield for Dr. Keeling. Dr. Wrench, of Baslow, was one of the first to arrive, and was soon afterwards followed by a medical gentleman from Hathersage. They could do but little, however, beyond confirming what was already known, that Miss Smith was dead, and that Mr. Littlewood's death must have been instantaneous, his death having been caused by a fractured skull, and also by probable serious internal injuries. As regards Mrs. Littlewood and Mdlle. Julien, it was considered desirable that they should return to Sheffield, and Dr. Keeling met their carriage as he was on his way to the scene of the accident. Mdlle. Julien was taken to Mr. Staniforth's residence on Northumberland Road, where she was attended by Dr. Keeling, and where she now lies. It was found that one of her legs was fractured above the knee, but the fracture is a simple one, and she is progressing favourably. Mrs. Littlewood's injuries are not fortunately of a serious character. The only fear is that *erysipelas* may set in.

The traction engine belongs to Mr. Sheard, the owner of a small colliery at Dronfield; and, singular to say, his son met his death only a few weeks ago by being run over by the same engine. Shortly after the accident Bailey had a conversation with the driver, in the course of which the latter said he did not hear anyone shouting just before the accident, and that the reason why he steered his engine away from the left-hand side of the road was that he might leave one of the trucks of coal at the Grouse Inn. This statement, of course, accounts for what at the time appeared a very extraordinary proceeding; for, as it has already been said, had he continued to keep the side of the road on which the engine was travelling when it was first seen, the accident could not have happened. At the time of the accident it was running tolerably rapidly, and the rattle of the wheels would doubtlessly make hearing difficult. No one connected with the engines was behind the trucks. A boy with a red flag was in front to warn vehicles of its approach, but that was all.

The bodies of Mr. Littlewood and Miss Smith remain at the Grouse Inn for the inquest. The former was twenty-one years of age. Miss Smith was but eighteen. She is an orphan, and the youngest of the two daughters of the late Mr. William Cook Smith, of Broomhall. Her sister is also a boarder at Miss Boaler's school. The grief of the latter when informed of the melancholy termination of the pleasure trip upon which her sister had gone only a few hours before, can be readily imagined. Much sympathy will be felt for her and for Mr. and Mrs. Littlewood. Intelligence of the accident became known to all the pleasure seekers who drove into Derbyshire by way of Frogatt Edge; and the event, painful in its suddenness and the terrible character of its results, could not fail to cast a gloom over all who passed that way. It was not until late in the afternoon that tidings of the accident became known in Sheffield; and here, where Mr. Staniforth and Mr. Littlewood are well known and highly respected, the utmost sympathy with them was expressed. It is in fact, long since an accident so painful as this has occurred in the neighbourhood, or one which naturally awakens emotions so deep.'

It is extrordinary that the delicacy required in the descriptions of 'gentlewomen' in Victorian England was extended even to the gruesome demise of Miss Smith!

Ben Littlewood's chest tomb lies to the right of, and set back from, the imposing Nathaniel Phillips memorial, close to the Egyptian Arch.

Joseph Binns

Joseph Binns owned and drove a hackney coach, and died a horrible death as a result of an accident in which his coach crushed him, while driving from Bakewell into the city. The accident happened at a turning of the road below Totley, when the coach ran over some ganisters hidden in drifting snow, which overturned the coach and then fell on him. Two passengers with him were not hurt, but Mr. Binns himself had terrible injuries including broken ribs and a broken collar bone. He lingered in great pain for a day before dying: 'death terminating his sufferings'. He left a widow and a large family of young children.

Joseph's wife, Jemima, took over the running of the family hackney coach business, on top of the care of her large family. Joseph's gravestone, a chest tomb, burial plot number H169, is to be found six plots to the left of the path leading up the hill to the Cemetery Office, three plots further up the hill from the retaining wall end. He died on 12th February 1841.

Gruesome Industrial Accidents

Robert Berresford

A local newspaper reported the following on 31ˢᵗ October 1846: 'On Saturday 17ᵗʰ October a man named Robert Berresford, residing in Burgen Street, while employed in a stone quarry near Ecclesall, suffered such injuries by an accident as to cause his death yesterday. It appears that he was working on a piece of projecting stone, about eleven yards from the bottom of the quarry, when a quantity of earth and stone from above, gave way and fell upon him, precipitating him from the place where he stood to the bottom of the quarry. In the fall, his head caught another piece of projecting stone and caused a fracture of the skull. Three of his ribs were also broken and other injuries caused. He had been under the care of Mr. Wallard and survived until yesterday.

Robert's gravestone is in a highly inaccessible area, plot number G7.

Joseph Shaw

Reported in the *Sheffield and Rotherham Independent* on 28ᵗʰ August 1851: 'A youth, named Joseph Shaw, aged 14, died at the Infirmary on Wednesday night from injuries received on 12ᵗʰ August. Shaw was a comb buffer and worked at Ward's wheel, Arundel Street. On the 12ᵗʰ instant, while engaged in putting a band on a pulley, his right arm became entangled with the band, and was seriously fractured thereby. The sufferer was removed to the Infirmary where the arm was amputated and, as we have previously indicated, he died there on Wednesday night.'

The burial register shows that Joseph Shaw, 'an infant aged 13' died from 'amputation of an arm' on 27 August 1851 and was buried in public grave NN12, near the River Porter. His parents were Henry and Sarah Shaw.

John Pickering

A report headed *Death from the breaking of a Grinding-stone* appeared on 27ᵗʰ September 1844. Pickering, only 16 when the accident took place, was an apprentice to John Travis, file-grinder. The report states: 'It appeared that whilst the deceased was at his work, at the Castle Mills, the stone over which he was working broke, and some of the pieces striking him, he received some very severe internal injuries, from which he died.' The breaking of the stone was attributed, by some, to 'the deceased working with too small a pulley, and to Travis not having a sufficient number of pulleys to regulate them, according to the work they were doing. The Jury returned a verdict of Accidental death.'

Our records show that, tragically, three more members of this family died in the Sheffield Flood, twenty years later. These were John's brother William, who drowned aged 33, his sisters Elizabeth and Sarah Ann aged 24. (They had a pub at the bottom of Walkley Lane). John, Sarah and Elizabeth are buried in a private plot number G120, which is unfortunately inaccessible at present. Also memorialized on the stone, though not buried there, (as when he drowned in the flood his body was never found), was William. The gravestone lists their names and states 'Drowned in the Great Flood'. Of William the gravestone states. 'He was never found'.

Thomas Chadburn

'Fatal Accident from the Breaking of a Grinding-stone – An inquest was held yesterday, at the sign of the Ball, in Lambert Street, on the body of Thomas Chadburn, aged thirty-seven, who died from the concussion produced by injuries received in the head and spine, in consequence of his being ejected from his horsing by the breaking of a grinding stone into several pieces. Mary Chadburn, widow of the deceased, said, "My husband was a file grinder, and worked for Messrs Wragg and Blackwell, at Mr. Marshall's, the Tower Grinding Wheel, in Blonk Street. He left his home after dinner on Thursday, the 4th of April instant, to go to work, and was brought home between four and five o'clock, very much hurt." He died on Wednesday morning at quarter-past-one. Dr. Lennard, and Mr. Booth, surgeon, had both attended the deceased. Her husband told her he thought the wheel was going rather too fast, when the stone on which he was working broke, threw him off the horsing, and he fell on the drum. He did not blame anybody. He said he thought the men above were off work, and that the engine consequently went at a greater speed. The engine was lame, and another was put on which always went irregularly. Thomas Cousins, of Arundel Street, file grinder, stated that he works at the Castle Mills Grinding Wheel, and on Thursday week was working on the right side of the deceased when he heard a stone break. He saw it was the deceased's and he was thrown off the horsing on the drum board. He, assisted by Wm Chandler, bore him out, and accompanied him home. He was cut at the back of the head, and appeared very much hurt. He was thrown five or six yards. He could not say whether any one was to blame or not. The wheel had been going rather fast, but he could not say whether it was then or not. The stone was not a plated one, but he considered it safe. One engine fell lame on the Tuesday, and he thought the one that was working did not go

Where to find the graves

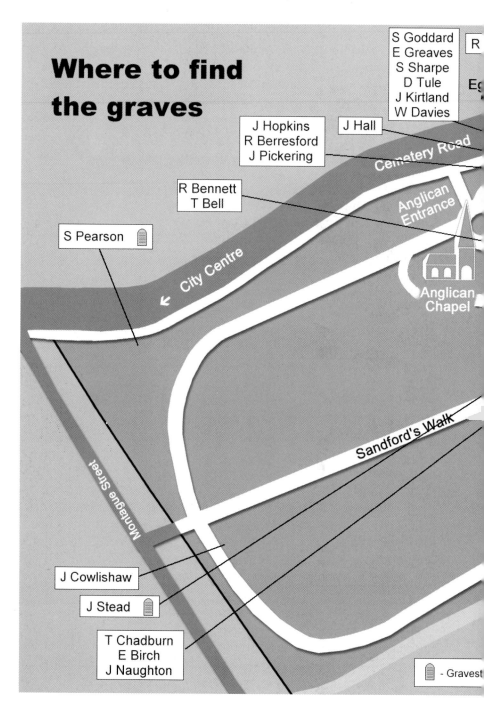

S Goddard
E Greaves
S Sharpe
D Tule
J Kirtland
W Davies

R

Eg

J Hopkins
R Berresford
J Pickering

J Hall

Cemetery Road

R Bennett
T Bell

Anglican Entrance

S Pearson

City Centre

Anglican Chapel

Sandford's Walk

Montague Street

J Cowlishaw

J Stead

T Chadburn
E Birch
J Naughton

- Gravest

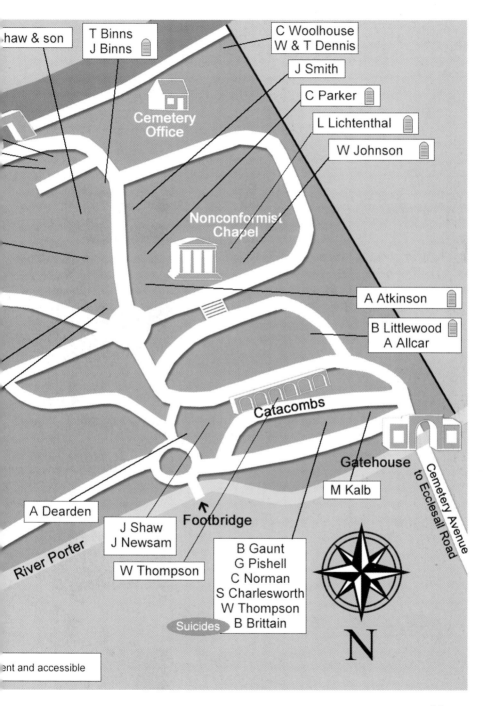

haw & son

T Binns
J Binns

C Woolhouse
W & T Dennis

J Smith

C Parker

L Lichtenthal

W Johnson

Cemetery
Office

Nonconformist
Chapel

A Atkinson

B Littlewood
A Allcar

Catacombs

Gatehouse

M Kalb

Cemetery Avenue
to Ecclesall Road

A Dearden

J Shaw
J Newsam

Footbridge

W Thompson

B Gaunt
G Pishell
C Norman
S Charlesworth
W Thompson
B Brittain

Suicides

River Porter

N

ent and accessible

35

quite so regularly as the other. They had never complained of it to Mr. Marshall. Some of the men were gone off to look at some fighting in the hull above ... William Chandler stated that he was in the room above, and hearing the alarm, came down and assisted Cousins to take the deceased home. He could not blame any person. A man named John Cocking had wished the stone would break the same morning, and knock his brains out, because he did not contribute to the Trade's Union; and yesterday, Cousins and he were going to see Chadburn, and passed Cocking, who was holing a stone. Cocking said to Cousins, "Well, I've got my wish, and I wish thine may break today, and serve thee the same" Cousins said, "I shall be no worse for that." He said, "I should like to break thy head with his hammer now." Cousins said, "Thou can't." Cocking said, "But I'll have a knife up to the haft in thee before I've done with thee." The deceased did not belong to the Union, nor Cousins either. Cocking belonged to the Union, and was on the box at the present time. The Coroner and Jury spoke in terms of the utmost condemnation of the inhuman and unChristian wishes expressed by Cocking. After the facts had been gone into at some length, the Jury returned a verdict of 'Accidental Death'.

Thomas Chadburn is buried in a public grave plot number V90, where there is now a clearing with a modern headstone at the central junction on the site.

Richard Robertshaw

A Fatal Boiler Accident was reported in which two men were killed. 'On Tuesday morning, about half-past eight, a frightful accident occurred at the saw manufactory of Mr. John Davenport, Rockingham Street, which has proved fatal to two individuals, whilst another was so seriously scalded, that for some time, but slight hopes were entertained of his recovery. The accident appears to have arisen from a defective bolt, which fastened a stop-valve placed at the top of a pipe communicating between the two boilers and the engine. Some repairs had been made at this point on the two previous days, and on Tuesday morning, observing a leakage of steam, the engine-tenter, whose name was Richard Robertshaw, stopped the machinery by fastening down the valve, and then proceeded to remedy the defect by screwing more tightly the bolts which secured it to the pipe. Whilst so engaged, the head of one of the bolts gave way, and the power of the steam was forced off the "bonnet" of the valve, and notwithstanding that Robertshaw gave instant alarm, two of the men, named Daniel Wilkins and John

Crookes, who were standing in the boiler-room at the time were dreadfully scalded before they could make their escape. A third man, named Latham, having a moment before, observed that one of the standards of the valve was broken, and fearful of an accident, was proceeding out of the room when the accident occurred, and thereby escaped the fate of the rest. Robertshaw, who was standing close to the spot, was scalded the worst, and died while being removed to his house, a few yards instant. Wilkins, who was standing in the doorway leading from the engine-room to the boiler-room, was also very dreadfully scalded. He made his way into the engine house, and was found after the accident, lying at the bottom of an excavation in which the fly wheel works. He and Crookes, who was also seriously injured, were afterwards removed to the Infirmary, where Wilkins died the same afternoon. Crookes is likely to recover, though very slowly.'

The inquest was held the day after the incident, and the scene of the accident was visited. Latham, described as a *snuff brusher*, said he had called at the engine-house and then at the boiler-house on the morning of the accident. In the boiler-house he saw Robertshaw standing on the steam-pipe, screwing down the stop-valve. He continued, 'After having knocked in two wedges between the joint belonging to the "bonnet" of the valve, he asked witness for a spanner, and on obtaining it, he began to tighten the stop-valve joint, in order to prevent the steam from escaping. Not being able to do it alone, Robertshaw requested John Crookes, who was standing by, to assist him. He gave the nut about half a turn, and then went to the bolt on the other side, and prepared to tighten that also. Whilst doing so, witness perceived that one of the standards belonging to the valve was broken, and called Robertshaw's attention to the fact, who replied that he knew about it. Fearing danger, witness immediately moved towards the fire-hole door, and had scarcely reached it when he heard Robertshaw call out that the bolt had stripped. On this, he immediately leaped from the top steps into the fire-hole, and escaped without injury, save a slight hurt on his arm. As he was leaving the steps, witness heard the "bonnet" fall, and the steam rush from the pipe, which filled the place directly and issued from the windows.'

Richard Robertshaw and his son (also killed in an accident) are buried in private plot number L158. The gravestone is currently inaccessible.

Precarious Exploits by Small Children

Edwin Birch

A cautionary tale was reported on 24th June 1843. 'On Monday afternoon, a boy named Edwin Birch, aged five years, and son of Thomas Birch, file cutter, Sheldon Street, was missed. Diligent search was made for him, but he was not found till Wednesday morning, when the body was discovered in the well of a garden, occupied by George Watson. The garden was about fifty yards from the house of the boy's father, and it is supposed that he got over the garden hedge, which was low, to catch a butterfly and stepped on the cover of the well, which had overturned, and let him in.'

Edwin is buried in a public plot (V66) which is in the clearing near the central junction on the site.

"He got over the garden hedge, which was low, to catch a butterfly and stepped on the cover of the well, which had overturned, and let him in."

William Frances Davies

Reported on 27th June 1840, headed *Uncovered Wells*. 'An inquest was held before Mr. Mandell, of Doncaster, on Wednesday, at the Broomhall Tavern, Broomhall Street, on the body of a boy named William Francis Davies, aged four years. The father of the child resides in Bath Street, and is a joiner, working at a building in Broomhall field, belonging to Mr. Caukwell. The child went with his father, when he returned from dinner, to work, on Monday, played about for some time, but about four o'clock was found drowned in a well, which was open in the back part of the premises. The father saw him at about half past two, but soon afterwards missed him and supposed he had gone to school. There were bricklayers working within a few yards of the place, but no one saw him fall into the well. The jury felt it to be their duty to express disapprobation of a custom, which is far too common, of persons leaving their wells open and unguarded during the erection of buildings, for the use of which they are intended.'

William is buried in public plot number B69, close to the Egyptian Gate in the fenced off area.

Arthur Allcar

Little Arthur Allcar's accidental death was reported on 28th November 1846. 'On Wednesday an inquiry was held ... at the New Market Hotel, Sheaf Street, on the body of Arthur Allcar, a little boy of not quite two years old who died on Tuesday in consequence of injuries rendered by falling from a chamber window. It appeared that on the Friday previous, the child's parents had gone out leaving it in the care of a sister, a girl ten years of age. She stated that she had the child on the dressing table in the chamber, and the window open. She took the child off the table, closed the window and fastened it with a hesp. Whilst she was playing in the room, the child climbed on the table and unfastened the hesp which fitted very loosely. The weight of his body against the casement forced it to open, and he fell from the window into the street. Medical aid was obtained, but the injuries were of such a severe nature, that the child never spoke afterwards, and died on Tuesday morning.

We have not been able to find Arthur's gravestone, but it is private plot LL42, which means there is usually a headstone, and lies close to the Egyptian arch and at the top of the slope that runs down steeply to the main path from the land above.

William Johnson

Reported in 18th July 1840 'T. Badger Esquire held an inquest at the Fitz-william Hotel, touching the death of a little boy, about four years of age, the son of Mr. Johnson, manufacturer, Fitzwilliam Street. It appears that on Saturday evening, the servant had put the deceased and two other children to bed in the garret, and when she had left them, they got up to the window. The deceased pulled down the upper sash, which ascended with a jerk, and the poor child fell out. He fell upon the pointed palisades before the house, and one of the points entering his body and another his head, and he was killed on the spot, instantaneously.'

Unfortunate little William is buried in private plot DD65, along with his sister, who also died young. You can find this low stone at the top of the steps in front of the Nonconformist chapel steps. Facing the chapel, turn right, pass the large column with railings, and you will find this stone a couple along, set back. The memorial inscription is on the triangular end of the monument as you face it.

Benjamin Brittain

A Fatal Accident was reported on 6th September 1845. 'An enquiry was held at the office of T. Badger, coroner, on Wednesday evening, on view of the body of Benjamin Brittain, a boy aged nine years, son of Mr. Brittain, butcher. It appeared in evidence, that on the previous afternoon, the deceased, who was residing with his grandfather, a person named Tomlinson, in Burnt Tree Lane, was playing with some other boys, near his grandfather's house, when in running after another boy, through a passage leading from Matthew Street to Hoyle Street, the other boy lifted up the handle of a pump, which was in the middle of the passage and the deceased, who was running very fast, caught his head against it and fell insensible to the ground. He was removed to his grandfather's, and medical assistance sent for, but he did not survive more than an hour.'

Benjamin is buried in private plot RR168, in front of the catacombs, the headstone has gone.

A Miscellany of
Distressing Circumstance

Stephen Pearson

'A serious stabbing case took place in Sheffield at an early hour this morning, as the result of which, it is feared, the life of an officer of the Borough Police Force is endangered. It appears that a navvy, named Peter Byrne, a stranger to the town, was hanging about and creating some disturbance in the Haymarket. The attention of the police was attracted to the man, and Police Constable Stephen Pearson (234) requested him to move on. The fellow refused, and on the officer attempting to arrest him Byrnes struck at him with a knife, inflicting a terrible gash in the officer's face. The knife cut through Pearson's helmet, and laid bare the cheek bone from below the ear to the chin. J Booth, of Duke Street, went to the officer's assistance, and they conducted the man to the Central Police Station, where he was handed over to other hands. Immediately on Pearson reaching the station he fell in a faint from loss of blood. Police Constable Bailey, the turnkey, did what he could for the injured man, and a cab was procured in which he was removed to the Dispensary. One rumour had it that Pearson was also stabbed in the neck, that the jugular vein was severed, and that he was not expected to reach the Dispensary alive. This statement, however, was an exaggeration, though there is no doubt that the injuries are of a serious character. After thus violently assailing the officer, Byrne threw away the knife. It was recovered, however, and proves to be of rather peculiar construction, consisting of a sharp razor blade in an ordinary knife shaft. Inquiries at the Hospital on the moment of going to press indicate that there is no immediate danger, although the wound is one of considerable depth, and the loss of blood was great.'

In fact, Stephen died a few months later, on 18th June 1892 - perhaps septicaemia had set in? His headstone records the stabbing as his cause of death with the words 'stabbed in Castle Street'. It can be found against the wall that backs on to Cemetery Road, behind the shrubbery that lies between the path going down the hill and the wall, about two thirds of the way down the sloping path from the Anglican chapel.

Mary Kalb

Infant Strangled was the heading on the news report in the Sheffield Times on 16th October 1847. 'An inquest was held on the body of Mary Agatha Kalb, aged fourteen months, daughter of Mr. Kalb of Hermitage Street, comb maker. It appeared that the family are natives of the Tyrol, in Austria, but have for some time been resident in Sheffield. The child had several times fallen out of bed onto the floor, by which it had severely injured itself, and in order to prevent such a repetition of this, its father fastened a strap to the bed and buckled it to the child's dress. On Monday afternoon, at three o'clock, the infant was put to bed, and secured in the manner described, when it must have attempted to get up, and was accidentally strangled by the strings of its dress being drawn too tight around its neck. At about five o'clock, when its mother went to see it, she found it hanging over the bedside completely dead. The infant was the only child of its parents and evidence was adduced which showed that they had ever treated it with the greatest fondness and affection.

Mary is buried in private plot SS176, close to the river, but any headstone there may have been has now gone.

"Evidence was adduced which showed that they had ever treated the child with the greatest fondness and affection"

Thomas Bell

Death By Choking – A singularly distressing circumstance took place in West Field Terrace on Wednesday last. Mr. Bell, a retired officer of the excise, was in the act of dining, when a bone or large piece of meat lodged in his throat. Medical assistance was immediately sent for to the Dispensary, when a medical gentleman, in the absence of Mr. Law, hastened to his relief. Most unhappily for the suffering patient, no *probang* was to be found at the Dispensary, which would have afforded instant relief; and the unfortunate individual, after intense suffering, breathed his last. We are aware of the limited funds of the Dispensary, but the importance of having its surgical instruments complete, will, we are sure, be felt by the Board of that charitable establishment. We are convinced that they will not willingly allow a deficiency of instruments, in an establishment where they are liable to be hourly called for.

Thomas Bell was 79 when he died on 6ᵗʰ March 1841 and 'deservedly respected'. He is buried in private plot S95. His grave is inaccessible.

James Smith

A news report published on 28ᵗʰ January 1880 was headed *Death of a Medical Student from the use of Chloroform.* 'A painful case, illustrative of the fatal effects of the incautious use of chloroform, occurred at Sheffield on Monday, the sufferer being Mr. James Smith, aged twenty-one, a pupil in the house of the late Mr. Jas. Ray, surgeon, and the third son of William Smith, Esq., of Dam House, barrister. On Sunday evening, Mr. Smith attended Divine service at St. Philip's church, and at its close accompanied Mr. Harwood, a son of Dr. Harwood, to that gentleman's residence, at Broom grove. After partaking of supper, Mr. Harwood walked with him as far as Mr. Ray's door, where they separated, after having made an appointment for the following evening. In consequence of the death of Mr. James Ray, several of the members of his family had come from a distance in order to attend the funeral, which took place on Saturday; and all the spare rooms of the house being occupied, a bed was made up in Mr. Smith's room for Mr. John Ray of Barnsley, the brother of the deceased gentleman. Mr. Smith retired to rest about half past eleven on Sunday night, and was followed by Mr. Ray about twenty minutes afterwards. He found that Mr. Smith had put out his light, and was apparently asleep. After Mr. Ray had been in bed about a quarter of an hour, he heard Mr. Smith moan, and in consequence, raised himself on the pillow, and listened attentively for a few minutes. As there was no repetition of the noise, he concluded that Mr. Smith had been dreaming, and accordingly composed himself to sleep. On waking the following morning, at about six o'clock, Mr. Ray arose, and while dressing called to Mr. Smith, but as he did not reply, and appeared to be asleep, no further attempt was made to disturb him. Mr. Ray observed that he lay in the same position as he had seen him the night before; that the bedclothes were comparatively undisturbed, and that Mr. Smith's face was partly concealed by the sheet. The family assembled for breakfast about half-past eight, when enquiry was made for Mr. Smith, who had not made his appearance. One of the domestics went up to his bedroom, the door of which she found wide open, and knocked loudly without receiving any answer. She walked to the bedside, and shook Mr. Smith by the shoulder, but failing to wake him, she ran down stairs and gave an alarm. Mr. Jackson, surgeon, whose house adjoins Mr. Ray's, was immediately called in, and he, on entering the room, found Mr. Smith upon his right side, quite dead. In his hands, he held a pocket handkerchief, which was firmly pressed to his mouth and nostrils. His knees were partially drawn up, and his limbs were in a state of rigid contraction. Mr. Smith, it appears, has for some time, been in the habit of inhaling chloroform, which he poured upon his handkerchief, and applied to the nostrils, for the purpose of allaying a severe pain in his face, to which he was subject.'

Mr. Henry Harwood, a good friend of Mr. Smith, gave evidence at the inquest. He said that Mr. Smith had told him many times that he was in the habit of taking chloroform to allay a severe pain in his face and head. He said he had met Mr. Smith on the Sunday before his death at the house of a friend. He found him 'reclining on a sofa, and complained, as he had done for two or three days before, of a pain in the face, and feeling unwell'.

A *post mortem* was carried out, and Mr. Jackson reported that 'The fact of his lying in a horizontal position while inhaling the chloroform, the head being almost entirely covered with bed-clothes, and his being unable, from insensibility, to remove the handkerchief, would produce the suffocation which resulted in death…I have no doubt that death resulted from incautiously inhaling chloroform.'

It is likely that Mr. Smith was suffering from trigeminal neuralgia, which can be an extremely painful condition affecting the trigeminal nerve that runs down one side of the face. Today, this condition can be treated effectively. Mr. Smith is buried in plot N2, in the group of graves behind the Nonconformist chapel in the fenced-off area. The grave is inaccessible.

Unsound minds

George Pishell
This sad story was reported on 4ᵗʰ November 1848. *'Love and Suicide.* An inquest was held on Tuesday evening at the Ball Inn, Shemeld Croft, on the body of George Pishell, aged twenty. From the circumstances which transpired in evidence, we learn that the deceased was a native of Germany, and an itinerant musician. He visited Sheffield for the first time, about a fortnight ago, and lodged at a house in Shemeld Croft, kept by a person named Middleton. Whilst an inmate there, he became acquainted with a young woman, named Margaret Crofts, also a native of Germany and following the same occupation as himself. Thrown into such close proximity it is not strange that they should feel a mutual interest in each other's welfare, as fellow pilgrims from their fatherland. This intimacy on the deceased's part soon ripened into love, and was so far reciprocated by the female, that before many days had elapsed, he obtained her consent, and the 'spurrings' were put in for their marriage. The deceased during this period was visited by his master, who resides in Leeds, whose services he had hastily left, to persuade him to return, but he expressed his determination to no longer follow his former calling, but to seek work in Sheffield. In this, he was supported by Crofts, who feeling herself ashamed to go out with music, considered it was far more degrading in a man, and accordingly she was desirous that he should change his employment. During the first few days after which this interview took place, she had an opportunity to observe the disposition of the man to whom she had pledged her hand, and to form an estimate of his character. Instead of seeking work he preferred to remain in idleness at home. The girl, during this time, relieved his wants, or he would have been utterly destitute. But seeing how slight was the hope of happiness she would derive from a union with a man who was both idle and bad tempered, she at length withdrew her former pledge, and offered him money to enable him to return to his master, but he said he would rather drown himself than do so. This was on Sunday night, when he had been more than usually noisy and troublesome, insomuch that he was turned out of his lodgings. During Monday he was very low-spirited, and to his companions expressed his determination to destroy himself if Margaret Crofts would not marry him. On Tuesday morning, at about 11 o'clock, he again sought her presence to see if she would alter her mind, but she told him that her opinion was unaltered, and intimating her intention to return to her birthplace, Frankfurt-on-the-Main. She again offered him money in order to return to his former service, but as to marrying him, she

said she could not. He then left her greatly excited, and was seen shortly after by a young man of his acquaintance, named George Pear, running up Baker's Hill, to whom he said, that he was going to pawn his coat, and then make away with himself. About 12 o'clock he was found by the same young man, whose suspicions were aroused by the excited manner of the deceased, suspended by his neckerchief to one of the spars of an outhouse appertaining to his lodgings. When found, his body was still warm, and life was not quite extinct; but before medical aid arrived he was quite dead. The young woman Crofts was commended by the coroner for her sensible and prudent conduct throughout the unfortunate affair. The Jury returned a verdict of temporary insanity.'
Pishell is buried in a public plot GG79, allotted to suicides, at the end of the catacombs.

Catherine Parker
It appears that poor Catherine Parker, wife of the exemplary Mr. Parker, cutlery exporter, took over the cares of the business on the death of her husband. She managed these business affairs, and those of her family, successfully till 1844, but once the business was wound up and her children 'advantageously settled', her health and mind gave way. It appeared that she began to suffer from the delusion that she had got the business in a financial muddle, believing that she could not even afford to pay a small sum for medication. She lost interest in her family 'She did not take as much notice of her grandchildren on Saturday morning as usual, and did not kiss them' her daughter Ellen testified at the inquest. Her accountant, Mr. Ebenezer Smith, said that she was 'very anxious about her religious state, and conceived that she had lost all her Christianity'. She had been heard to say 'I don't think I'm in a state of derangement, but of idiotcy….I have a strange undefined feeling, which much oppresses me.'
This confusion and hopelessness must finally have proved too much for the poor woman, as the sordid manner of her death described by her son Ebenezer at the inquest demonstrates. 'On Saturday morning, my mother breakfasted with my brother Elliott and my sister Ellen. I did not breakfast with them. While dressing, about nine o'clock, I heard two falls in the room above the chamber in which I was. It was in my brother's sleeping room, in the attic. I went upstairs in consequence of the falls and repeated groans, and found my mother lying on the floor. She was dead. There was an immense quantity of blood on the floor, and on a chest of drawers,

and likewise on her dress. She had destroyed herself with a razor belonging to my brother Elliott, which she had taken off a chest of drawers. He had slept in that room, and was just gone out after breakfast to Smith and Wrightman's office, with whom he is articled. I made an alarm, and my brother George came. I took the razor out of my mother's right hand. The grasp was relaxed. It was bloody.'

Thus this poor woman, whose life ended in madness and violent death at the age of fifty-three, is not memorialized with her husband on the grandest monument in the cemetery, but more discretely, on a tablet stone to the left of the Nonconformist chapel, at the rear.

"She had destroyed herself with a razor belonging to my brother Elliott, which she had taken off a chest of drawers."

Aaron Dearden

A news report of 3rd July 1879 reports the *Shocking Suicide of Mr. Aaron Dearden, a suicide of a very distressing character.* He worked for the firm of Messrs Rodgers and Dearden of the Philadelphia Corn Mills, and occupied the premises of this firm just below the Dale Dyke dam in Bradfield. When the dam burst the house and mill were flooded. The paper states: 'Mr. and Mrs. Dearden sought refuge on the roof of the house where they remained until the water had subsided. Mr. Dearden's anxiety for his family together with the violent cold he caught by the exposure, told very seriously on his health. He subsequently removed into Albert Terrace Road, and it is a remarkable fact that year by year, as the anniversary of the flood came round, he was attacked with a depression of spirits which sometimes left him in a very weak state. So regularly did the affliction come upon him that he used to speak of it as his *annual attack of flood fever*. Two years ago he lost his wife; and some six months after his mills were destroyed by fire.'

The paper continues: 'These and other disquieting circumstances of a private nature further affected his spirits, and his attack of *flood fever* this year left him more prostrate than usual. A friend who called to see him a month ago found him in a most desponding state, and in the course of the conversation, he remarked that he felt really tired of his life. Instead of getting better his depression rather increased. On Tuesday night this was very much the case, and shortly before he went to bed he told his daughter that if he did not feel better in the morning he should call in Dr. Roberts, who had attended him previously. Yesterday morning between eight and nine o'clock, his daughter went to his bedroom, for the purpose of taking him his breakfast, and was horrified to find that her father was not in bed, but was lying partly on the floor, his neck tied with his handkerchief to one of the posts at the foot of the bed.'

We will spare you the details of the gruesome description of his death, written up in the newspaper in lavish detail. Mr. Dearden was, by the paper's account, universally respected and took a keen interest in everything related to Nether Hallam. He was about 55 years old. Dearden is buried in a public plot (MM127) near the River Porter, next to the footbridge that crosses it.

Charles Norman

The following suicide was reported on 25th March 1854. 'On Thursday T. Badger, coroner, held an inquest at the Loch Lomond Inn, Eyre Street, on the body of Charles Norman, aged 53, cabinet case maker, who committed suicide on Tuesday evening. The deceased was employed by Messrs Russell and Jackson of Norfolk Street, and resided with his wife in Norfolk Lane. He had been for a number of years in the Spanish Army and during that time suffered from afflictions of the liver, stomach, and the back. His pains were so severe that he was unable to sleep, or remain in bed for other than a very short period. He was under the care of Mr. Samuel Gregory, surgeon. The pain and loss of rest seemed to have affected deceased's mind. A few days ago he remarked to his wife that unless confined, he should do something desperate; and at times appeared very wild and flighty. Between eight and nine o'clock on Tuesday evening he went home in a very depressed state and asked his wife to fetch him a penny worth of ale. She went, and on her return in about five minutes found the deceased lying on the floor with his razor in his hand and his throat terribly cut. She gave an alarm and the deceased immediately placed the razor upon a table which was within his reach. Surgeons were called in but death ensued in about an hour afterwards. Verdict: suicide during temporary insanity.'

Charles is buried in a public burial plot number RR132, in front of the catacombs.

Benjamin Gaunt

A Melancholy Case of Self-Destruction was reported on 7th May 1853.

'- mainly caused, as the circumstances will show, by over anxiety in respect of some building transactions in which the deceased has been engaged. He was a scale cutter, and formerly resided in St Philips Road. He was steady and industrious, held strong religious views, and was a member of the Howard Street Chapel. On the formation of the Freedom Hill Building Society, he became a member, and since then had been most anxious to erect a house on the estate. To accomplish this object he worked early and later, and a fortnight ago he removed his wife and four children to a house he had built in Palm Street, Freedom Hill. During the time the house was being built, the deceased was much harassed in his mind, and after his removal to it, his children, who were poorly before, became worse. This, and the damp, unfinished state of the house, increased his unhappiness. He was also greatly distressed by a conviction that in his anxiety to build, he had neglected his religious duties. His intellect gave way under its accumulated burdens. He ceased to work on Friday last, and on the following Tuesday, symptoms of mental aberration were apparent. He fancied that he and his family were going to the workhouse, and even asked his wife to fetch a cab to take them there. During Tuesday night he became particularly violent, and about half past twelve, sprung out of bed, and attempted to strangle his wife and children, and also himself. His wife providentially succeeded in staying his hand, though, in his attempt on her life, he inflicted very serious injury on her neck. All night she remained alone with the madman. She called for help, but no one heard her cries, and she durst not leave the house a moment lest he should do some violence in her absence.

As it was, he made a second attempt on his life, and being prevented by his wife, he endeavoured to set the house on fire. Ever since then, he has been constantly watched, the neighbours kindly rendering the wife every assistance. Once he tried to make his way into the garret and throw himself from a small window which overlooks the garden, but was frustrated. He continued in a delirious state up to Thursday morning, when taking advantage of his wife's absence from the room, he got up from his bed and ascended into the garret. His wife returned instantly after, and missed him from the room. She had not sufficient strength of mind to follow him, but ran to the door, and called to Mrs. Cryor, who lived in the adjoining house. Mrs. Cryor came immediately, and just arrived to see the deceased drop from the window to the ground, a distance of twenty seven feet. No bones were broken by the fall. After being removed to the house, he became so violent, that it took three men to restrain him, and sometime, when he appeared to be dead, he put forth almost super-human strength, setting at naught the efforts of the men to restrain him. He died about an hour after the accident. Mr. Skinner, surgeon, stated that the deceased had been labouring under delirium, arising from over-fatigue and anxiety, and had died from the shock caused by the fall, the act having been committed whilst labouring under temporary insanity.'
Benjamin Gaunt is buried in public plot PP16, in the area in front of the catacombs.

Samuel Charlesworth
Samuel Charlesworth, of Hillfoot, was a tall, fine-looking young man, nearly twenty-five years of age. He was a file cutter, employed by Marsh and Shepherd's. The news report of 12th April 1845 tells a sad tale: 'the evidence adduced before the jury went to shew, that when the deceased became of age, and for some time after, he became very wild and dissipated in his habits, which continued until about a year ago, since which time he had been in the most depressed spirits, and apparently not of sound mind. About nine months ago, his mother, to whom it appears he was most fondly attached, was taken dangerously ill, and after a short illness died. This circumstance appeared to increase the depression of spirits under which he laboured, and that depression was still further increased by a respectable young female, to whom he had formed a most ardent attachment, and to whom, but for his untimely death, he was to have been married next Monday, being about this time taken ill, and her life despaired of. She,

however, after a long illness recovered, but from the evidence of his father and sister, it appeared that he never afterwards regained his former buoyancy of spirits, and appeared careless as to the manner in which he performed his work, and to all objects around. About two months ago, he left his home for a day or two, without assigning any reason, or saying where he was going to; and when he returned home he told his relations that he had been wandering around the neighbourhood of Chesterfield, and on his way home again, he went into a wood, near Coal Aston, with the intention of hanging himself, but when about to commit this rash act, his mother's ghost appeared in a flash of fire, and warned him not. About this time, he was walking with his intended wife, when they met some female, with who they were both acquainted, and when about parting, he bid her goodbye, saying that she would not see him again. The young woman said, in a joking manner, that she supposed he meant that she should not see him again single; and he answered, 'No, not alive'. He afterwards, when asked what he meant by using such words, said that he was only jesting. About ten o'clock on Thursday morning, he left home, apparently in his usual health and spirits, and in about half an hour from that time, he went to the shop of Mr. Henry Spalton, druggist, in Infirmary Lane, and said he had taken an ounce of mercury, and wanted a stomach pump to be applied. Mr. Spalton thought that if the man's statement was correct, he ought to take him to a surgeon, and accordingly took the deceased to Mr. Payne, and as that gentleman was not in at that time, he took him to the infirmary, and left him there, in the care of Mr. Law, the house-surgeon. On the way to Mr. Payne's, the deceased told Mr. Spalton that he had had by him two months the poison he had taken, and that he had before attempted to hang himself, and wished he had succeeded. The deceased made some statement to Mr. Law which he had previously made to Mr. Spalton, and produced two pieces of paper, on one of which was written 'arsenic – care', and on the other 'arsenic – poison'. Vomiting was immediately excited, and when the stomach had been emptied by those means, he appeared much better, and wished to go home. With some trouble however, he was persuaded to remain in the house, and went to lay down on one of the wards. Revill, one of the porters in the institution, accompanied the deceased to the ward, and in conversation which Revill had with him, he told him he wondered he had not thought better of himself than to commit such a rash act; in answer to which the deceased said he had something on his mind for a long time, but should not say what. He said he had taken an ounce of arsenic, which people said was sufficient to kill a dozen persons, but it appeared it would not do for him, and he should take other means. About four o'clock Mr. Law was summoned to him, and found him in a dying state, and he almost immediately expired. At the time when he wished to leave the house, in answer to a question from Mr. Law, he most pertinaciously refused to say where he had got the poison, as, he said, it might do the man harm. He said he would rather be silent as to his reasons for taking the poison, but eventually said he had been very dissipated and wild, kept very bad company, and had contracted disease. During the last twelve months, he had been quite steady, but his disease continuing, he grew low spirited, and considered himself unfit for society, and that was the reason he had taken the poison. In the post mortem examination by Mr. Law, the stomach was found highly inflamed, and that gentleman was of opinion, from the state in which the stomach was found, and the absence of disease in other important organs, that death had been caused by some corrosive or acrid poison being taken into the stomach. No appearances were found of any existing disease of the character which the deceased said he had contracted. The jury returned a verdict that the deceased died from having taken arsenic, being, at the time, of unsound mind.'

Charlesworth is buried in the public plot reserved for suicides in front of the catacombs, number SS175.

John Kirtland

The news reports of 27th March 1841 were headed *'Suicide by a traveller'*. 'On Saturday last a gentleman of the name of John Kirtland, a commercial traveller, committed suicide at the George and Commercial Inn, Market Place, Sheffield. He has travelled on commission for many years and has been in the habit of visiting Sheffield for two or three years, being well known to many respectable tradesmen, and has a large family, who are left to deplore his untimely end. An inquest was held on the body on Tuesday last, at the George Inn, before Mr. Badger, and a respectable Jury, when the following evidence was produced.

Mr. Edmund Smith deposed – I am landlord of the George Inn, Sheffield. I have known Mr. Kirtland for nearly three years, during which time he has come to my house about every four months. He comes from London, and is a commercial traveller, for the house of Messrs Lyons in the paper hanging and floor cloth business in Old Kent Road, opposite Surrey Square, London. He came to my house on Tuesday night last from Nottingham. He appeared quite sober, and in as good health as ever I saw him since I knew him. He went out on Wednesday morning to his customers: he returned in the evening, and had tea. I was not at home on Thursday, but I saw him in the house on Friday, about one o'clock, and he appeared as usual. We had dinner together in the parlour, along with four other persons, about a quarter past one. He had some gin and water after dinner, and then went out to do business. During the afternoon, I saw him three or four times. He came in that night about eleven o'clock. He had had liquor, but he was not drunk. I should say he was what is called *fresh*. He was not sober. He asked for a bed candle, and said he would go to bed. I had no other talk with him. He appeared in point of mind as well as I ever saw him in my life and had been steadier this journey than I had ever seen him before. He has been in the habit of getting tipsy. I should say when tipsy he knew what he was doing – it only made him talkative, but nothing more. About a quarter past two yesterday, when I was informed that he (Mr. Kirtland) had not got up, I called the waiter, fearing that something was amiss: I went and knocked at his bedroom door. He asked from within, 'Who's there?' I told him it was Mr. Smith, the landlord, and requested him to open me the door, and he said he was coming directly. I waited a minute or two; he did not open the door, and I looked through the keyhole, and saw Mr. Kirtland sat on the floor, and he appeared as if he was bleeding. I told him if he did not open the door, I should break it open. He did not open it, and I immediately set my foot against the door, and smashed it open. On entering his bedroom, I found him on the floor with his back against the wall, bleeding from his throat, which was cut in two or three places. I sent for Mr. Gregory, surgeon. He had only his shirt on - the bed or bedclothes were not bloody. I think he had cut his throat while on the floor with a knife which I found near him on the floor. The knife was bloody. His bedroom floor was locked inside, and the key in the inside. I do not think anyone had been in the room. His shirt was covered with blood. He lived about forty minutes after I found him. He appeared sensible when I spoke to him. We found a bottle in the room, now produced by Mr. Gregory. He appeared more a man of business this journey than I have before seen him. (The knife was then produced. It is what is called a Wharncliffe knife and was covered with blood.)

Mary Driver, chambermaid, confirmed the evidence of Mr. Smith as to deceased going in liquor to bed on Friday night in consequence of which she went about twelve o'clock to see if his candle was out, and found it was. At eight in the morning, his shoes and hot water were taken up, and twice during the morning enquiry was made at his room door if he was up, and he answered. At length witness looked through the keyhole and saw him sitting bleeding on the floor. She immediately informed Mr. Smith.

Mr. S. Gregory, surgeon, was sent for, and found the deceased in a bed-room, sat on the floor, with his back against the wall, and about a pint of blood on the floor beside him. On examination, I found two wounds in the neck, which had ceased bleeding. He told me he had taken about three ounces of laudanum about eleven o'clock the night before. He gave me no reason for his having done so, except that he said 'he wished to die.' He appeared to be collected, and knew what he was saying. I did not ask him where he got the laudanum. I found a bottle which had contained lau-danum, which is on the label, in legible characters, and the name of John Teers, druggist, Leicester, also on the label. I remained with him till he died, about an hour after I first saw him. I sewed up the wounds in his neck. I immediately sent for the stomach pump, and applied it without effect. If he had taken laudanum as he stated, the night before, at eleven o'clock, he must have been dead before the event. His pulse was nearly gone when I arrived. In my opinion he died from the effects of the laudanum and from the injuries to the throat, which were not of a fatal character, and not the proximate cause of death.

By a Juryman: He appeared quite rational, and resisted the introduction of a stomach pump. He said several times, 'Let me die; I wish to die;' in a calm manner.

Mr. W.V.Radley, druggist, proved that the deceased purchased four ounces of laudanum from him on Friday afternoon, when they had some conversa-tion as to the price of laudanum and its effects. He spoke of it as being for a female who took great quantities of it for a complaint. He appeared rational, sober in his manner, and not at all singular.

Richard Neaves, waiter at the George, had known deceased for some time, and saw no alteration in his manner. He corroborated the other witnesses as to the deceased drinking liquor before going to bed, and the breaking into his room the next day. While Mr. Smith was gone for a surgeon, he asked him if he knew what he had done, and he said 'yes, I have cut my throat with that knife', pointing to the one on the floor. He was in his night-shirt and cap. He asked for something to drink; I said I could not give him anything until the surgeon came, and he said 'It was drink that had done it and not him.' I found a bottle which had contained laudanum on the dressing table, which I gave to my master.

By a Juryman: He said nothing about his wife and his children. I said 'I am afraid you will die.' He said 'I am ready to die.' I said 'I am afraid you are not prepared to die.' He said in the bar the day before he had eleven daughters.

At the suggestion of the coroner, the inquest was adjourned to Tuesday, to give time for the friends of the deceased to arrive.

At the adjourned inquest William Fowler of West Street, cabinet maker, proved that he had known the deceased nine years, and had done business with him on his journeys to Sheffield. He called the witness on Thursday afternoon, and seemed greatly dejected. He carried a parcel of patterns, which I had never seen him do before. I did not give him an order, nor did he press for one. I advised him to take the omnibus, but he said he really could not afford it, - trade was so bad, he had scarcely taken an order all day. I remarked a change in his manner and conduct, and afterwards talked of it with my wife.

Mrs. Ann Miller, widow, West Street, cabinet maker, proved that she had known deceased eight years. Saw him on Thursday morning, when he did not appear to be himself. He was very silent, though he used to be very talkative. He sat down, but shewed me no articles, and I examined his patterns by myself. He appeared very low, and shed a tear or two as he sat. He seemed scarcely able to write the order I gave him.

Mr. James Kirtland, of Manchester, son of the deceased, proved that his father's name was James Sayer Kirtland, his age fifty or fifty-one. On the last two occasions that I have seen him in Manchester, he has been subject to great excitement, and delirious, which caused us much uneasiness. When questioned about it, he attributed it to the state of his trade, and losses which had swallowed up the little savings on which he had depended upon for the support of his old age. He travelled on commission, and his business had failed to pay his expenses. He has of late been an altered and dejected man. The jury found that the deceased had destroyed himself in a state of temporary insanity.'

Kirtland is buried in a public grave plot (B66) close to the Egyptian Gate.

John Yeomans Cowlishaw

In January 1895 the death of John Cowlishaw was reported, which had occurred under the 'most distressing circumstances'. News of his death spread rapidly throughout the city, especially in business circles, and 'created the most profound astonishment and deep sympathy'. Suffering from depression since the death of his wife fifteen months earlier, on the morning of 23rd January, Cowlishaw shut himself in the lavatory of his home at Tapton Cliffe and shot himself in the head with a sporting gun. He died instantly. By the time he died, aged sixty-five, he had built up an outstanding reputation as a silver knife manufacturer, specializing in silver fruit knives and was also well known as an art lover and patron of art. He was by then extremely wealthy, 'appeared to have everything he could wish – a splendid home, filled with the choicest art treasures, and rich beyond anything that he could possibly need' though sadly in his deep depression believed he was poor and would end up in the workhouse.

The circumstances of his death were as follows: 'He seemed to have been restless during the night, and rang up one of the servants to make him some tea. He was called as usual about half past seven yesterday morning, but did not get up until a little later. When he came down to breakfast he seemed better and altogether more cheerful than he was on the previous night. Some little time afterwards he went upstairs, and was seen on the landing by one of the servants with a double barrelled gun in his hand. He was accustomed to keep this gun under his bed, and no special alarm was created by his being seen with it near his room door. A short time after, the servants, who were in the kitchen, heard a noise….but they dismissed it and carried on with their tasks. About half an hour later the waiting maid, Elizabeth Clark, went in search of him as a doctor had arrived and wished to talk to him. She couldn't find him anywhere, and had knocked at the door of the water closet and received no answer. She was sent back to double check whether he was in the lavatory, and this time, receiving no reply, she tried the door and found that it was open. She looked in, and to her great horror saw Mr. Cowlishaw in a corner of the lavatory, with blood streaming from his head.' The left side of his head was completely shattered, and the gun was close by him.

He was John Newton-Mappin's nephew, the wealthy Sheffield brewer and art collector. John Mappin's first job had in fact been designing pearl handles for silver fruit-knives under his father, Joseph Mappin. Later Cowlishaw joined him. In 1854, Cowlishaw established his own business on Norfolk Street as a silver fruit-knife maker and pearl cutter. When Mappin retired Cowlishaw bought his silver and pearl business and combined it with his own. His obituary stated 'The concern had always been a prosperous one and Mr. Cowlishaw had always enjoyed a high reputation for the quality of his manufactures.' Today his knives are still regarded as outstanding, the best that Sheffield makers could produce in the nineteenth century.

Cowlishaw was on the board of many Sheffield businesses, and was also an avid art collector. When Mappin bequeathed his art collection to the city, Cowlishaw joined the Art Gallery committee and became a well respected member of it. He gave pictures to the gallery and loaned more, and also part-financed the construction of the Museum and Weston Park. The firm he established was still in existence in 1974. He left three sons.

Cowlishaw was buried in the Anglican area that has now been cleared, so his stone, now gone, would have been near the Montague Street entrance to the site. Much of this information regarding Cowlishaw was gleaned from The Sheffield Knife Book *by Geoffrey Tweedale published by the Hallam-shire Press, the rest from news reports.*

'She looked in, and to her great horror saw Mr. Cowlishaw in a corner of the lavatory, with blood streaming from his head.'

William Thompson
News reports of the 19ᵗʰ August 1901 described a *Sensational Suicide on the Railway*. The Fireman of the two-thirty Sheffield to Chesterfield train reported to the signalman that a man had been run over near Heeley station, and that his arm had apparently been cut off. The authorities at the station were immediately informed and a party was sent out to remove the body to a waiting room, while awaiting the arrival of a doctor. Once examined, he was rapidly dispatched to the Royal Hospital in an ambulance but died shortly afterwards. The man remained unidentified overnight, and the following description was released to the press:
'He is of stout build, about fifty five years of age, five feet six inches high, with dark hair, turning grey. The clothing included a dark check suit, a green and white check cap, and brown and white striped shirt. In the pockets were found two pawn tickets, a knife, pocket case, pair of spectacles in a case, and several needles. The latter would suggest that the deceased was a tailor by trade.' He was subsequently identified as William Thompson, tailor, and an inquest was held into his death. He was a tailor, aged forty-five, who had been lodging at 185, Broomhall Street. 'Deceased sustained fatal injuries by being run over by a Midland railway train near to Heeley station on Sunday afternoon – Albert Smith, with whom deceased had lodged for the last three weeks, said that deceased had been of intemperate habits. He was frequently drunk. Deceased had said that he was a native of Loughborough and was a tailor by trade. He had been employed in Sheffield, however, as a sewing machine agent, but had been dismissed from his employment, owing to his drunken habits. Witness last saw him alive on Saturday morning in the Fitzwilliam Hotel, and subsequently heard nothing of him until he saw the paragraph in yesterday morning's paper. Deceased had not actually said at any time that he would commit suicide, but he had several times said as he left the house that he would never come back. William Poole said that he was the stoker on the two-thirty p.m. train from Sheffield to Chesterfield on Sunday afternoon. As the train approached Heeley station he was hanging over the side of the engine, when he saw the deceased approach the line on his hands and knees and lay himself on the ground on the line in front of the train. The engine struck him, knocking him clear of the line. The train pulled up in Heeley station, and witness informed the officials what had happened. In answer to a question from the coroner, Poole said that he was sure the deceased purposely laid himself across the line, and did not simply stumble over it in a drunken

state.' The verdict was suicide during a state of temporary insanity. *William Thompson is buried in public vault QQ, one of the only catacombs to be used.*

James Newsam

The press reported an *Extraordinary Suicide* on 29th March 1851 and published two letters written by Mr. Newsam, aged twenty-two, which led the jury to conclude that he had taken his own life. The letters were to his employer and to his aunt, as follows:

'Mr. Wright,

You may have for some time observed a change in my manner and conduct. I have been careless, inattentive to my duties, and thoughtless to a degree which I know well has tried your patience. I cannot help it; gradually one absorbing thought has obscured all my faculties, made me appear a fool, and has at last made me die. Did you ever feel what it was to have a hideous phantom continually before your eyes, acting as a thrall on all your energies? Perhaps not. Such is my case, and the transactions of the last few days have made the burden too heavy for me to bear. I thank you and Mrs. Wright for your kindness to me; but the love of self being the predominating feature in human nature, I cannot help it. You will see that I have chosen prussic acid for my executioner. I request you will take, from what my salary amounts to, what I have caused you to be a loser of; and now farewell. Send the letter on the table to the address; they are the best friends I have. J. Newsam.'

'Ere you receive this, dear aunt, I shall be no more. Nay, start not, but read to the end. Oh aunt, to tell you what I have suffered in the conflict of my mind, is impossible. But I am no longer able to withstand the torture, far worse than death, which for the last few months, I have suffered. Oh why has my God made me the victim of the phantom which has gradually been gaining ascendancy over me. You cannot understand what I mean, but it has been a shadow perpetually haunting me, thrusting itself into all my thoughts and actions – the thought that I should never be a credit to myself or friends. Oh, you cannot understand how that one thought perpetually before you day and night, awake and in your dreams, bows down and ties all the energies of the soul, makes you reckless of everything you do, deters you from your duty, and carries you to the grave! Gradually has this madness (for such it is) been coming on for some time, and now, but one short hour, and I shall be ....(left blank). I had a mother, a fond

doting mother, who is now with the angels of heaven above. Oh how my prayers have been to meet her again, far beyond the cares and troubles of this bad world – prayed, yes often I have prayed the dark night through, and earnestly, oh how earnestly, God, before whom I shall soon stand, alone knows. Why has he not answered me? Why has he hid his face from me? I will go to him and trust in his mercy. Do not grieve for my departure from you, a few short years passed in care and anxiety, and then all would have been over; rather rejoice for I sorrow not, for I have a firm faith in the mercy of my Saviour. To you my dear aunt, my best of friends, I leave the last act I shall require of you, to break the tidings to father and dear sisters, God bless them and you. My parent has much to blame himself for during his life, and is now old. May the Lord stand in his path, and shew him everlasting light. Poor Dick, I should have liked to have heard of him. God bless him! I cannot do anything right. My master has had occasion to scold me often lately, but I have not been able to help it. I might as well try to stay the course of a mighty river as of the phantom which is killing me. My books, clothes and desk, in which you will find only ten shillings and sixpence, I leave in your care. I cannot stop here. I wish for rest – eternal rest, and may God in his infinite mercy, grant it me. Father I cannot write to, nor sisters, for it would be too much for them to bear; but you have seen and become familiar with death, and to your care I commend my things. Mr. Wright may speak harshly of me; I deserve it; I cannot help it; I have tried; prayed to be able to do my duty in the state of life it has pleased him to call me, but I cannot. And now farewell for ever on this side the grave; and what is it? Oh death where is thy sting? Oh grave, where is thy victory? But we have now the victory through our Lord Jesus Christ. My death is a short one – prussic acid. Once more, aunt, dear dear friend, farewell. May we all meet again in joy that knows no ceasing, and where all is happiness and peace.'

James' father was an Anglican minister, and lived in Bristol. James had been taken on as an apprentice with a chemist and druggist named Mr. Wright, and hence had easy access to poisons. Mr. Wright attended the inquest and described James at work. 'He has conducted himself very satisfactorily with the exception of a liability to make mistakes. He has complained to me of what he conceived to be his deficient education, especially with regard to Latin; but I considered he had received a fair education. He was a man of more than ordinary talent. He was the quickest compounder of medicines I ever saw.' He went on: 'Mr. Newsam has for a length of time appeared very bewildered and absent, but more especially during the last week. I have frequently detected him making mistakes, and he has immediately expressed his sorrow for, and consciousness of the mistake, and promised to be more careful....I have often said to Mrs. Wright that I was sure he must be very unhappy; and he has occasionally alluded to some family circumstances, but in a very indistinct way. Mr. Hugh Wood, surgeon, attended the scene when James's body was discovered. In his opinion, 'James, having poured prussic acid into the glass, had then corked the vial and returned it to its case, placed the glass on the chair by the bedside, having then extinguished the light had got into the bed, covered himself with the clothes, and reached his hand to the glass, had swallowed the deadly poison, and having returned the glass to the chair, had fallen back, dead. Such was the rapidity with which the poison had acted, that he could not have taken it any other way. Had he taken it at the table, he would have fallen down dead before he could have reached the bed.'

One wonders what the allusion to family unhappiness was about, perhaps connected to his father? His father did not transport his son's body to Bristol for burial in the family plot. James is buried in public burial plot NN5.

"You will see that I have chosen prussic acid for my executioner."